ESSENTIAL
Low Fat

Contents

Introduction

With the current media interest in healthy living, no one can be unaware of the problems associated with a diet which contains too much fat. A high level of fat consumption can lead to obesity and all that it entails, like coronary disease, diabetes and even cancer.

Reducing the amount of fat in our diets is an effective way to lose weight, simply because the number of calories we consume will be less, as well as reducing the likelihood of contracting a serious disease. However, excluding fat completely from our diet is not the answer. It is important to remember that we all need to include a certain amount of fat in our daily intake of food if our bodies are to function properly. Essential fatty acids are needed to build cell membranes and for other vital bodily functions. Our brain tissue, nerve sheaths and bone marrow need fat, for example, and we all need to protect vital organs such as the liver, kidneys and heart.

Nutritionists recommend that we should aim to cut our intake of fat to 27—30% of our total daily calorie intake. If your average diet totals 2000 calories per day, then you should eat no more than approximately 75 g/2¾ oz of fat a day. As a guide, bear in mind that most people consume about 40% of their daily calories in the form of fat. Remember however, that if you

are being treated for any medical conditions, you must discuss with your doctor any changes you plan to make in your diet.

It is important when thinking of reducing your fat intake to make the distinction between saturated and unsaturated fats. Saturated fats are those which are solid at room temperature and are mainly found in animal products such as butter and cheese, high-fat meats, cakes, chocolate, potato crisps, biscuits, coconut and hydrogenated (hardened) vegetable or fish oils.

Unsaturated fats are usually liquids from vegetable sources, and while they are healthier than saturated fats, they are still fats. Your target should be a reduction to 8% of your daily calories in the form of saturated fats, with the remainder in the form of unsaturated fats.

One of the most beneficial yet simplest changes you can make to your diet is to change from full-fat milk, cream, cheese and yogurt to a low- or reduced-fat equivalent. Also eat lots of vegetables, not only are they nutritional but naturally low in fat too.

Beef, Water Chestnut & Rice Soup

Serves 4 • CALORIES PER SERVING: 205 • FAT CONTENT PER SERVING: 4.5 G

INGREDIENTS

350 g/12 oz lean beef (such as rump or sirloin)
1 litre/1 3/4 pints/1 quart fresh beef stock
1 cinnamon stick, broken
2 star anise
2 tbsp dark soy sauce
2 tbsp dry sherry
3 tbsp tomato purée (paste)
115 g/4 oz can water chestnuts, drained and sliced
175 g/6 oz/3 cups cooked white rice
1 tsp zested orange rind
6 tbsp orange juice
salt and pepper

TO GARNISH:
strips of orange rind
2 tbsp chives, snipped

1 Carefully trim away any fat from the beef. Cut the beef into thin strips and then place into a large saucepan.

2 Pour over the stock and add the cinnamon, star anise, soy sauce, sherry, tomato purée (paste) and water chestnuts. Bring to the boil, skimming away any surface scum with a flat ladle. Cover the pan and simmer gently for about 20 minutes or until the beef is tender.

3 Skim the soup with a flat ladle to remove any scum again. Remove and discard the cinnamon and star anise. Blot the surface with absorbent kitchen paper to remove any fat.

4 Stir in the rice, orange rind and juice. Season with salt and pepper to taste. Heat through for 2–3 minutes before ladling into warm bowls. Serve the soup garnished with strips of orange rind and snipped chives.

VARIATION

Omit the rice for a lighter soup that is an ideal starter for an Oriental meal of many courses. For a more substantial soup that would be a meal in its own right, add diced vegetables such as carrot, (bell) pepper, sweetcorn or courgette (zucchini).

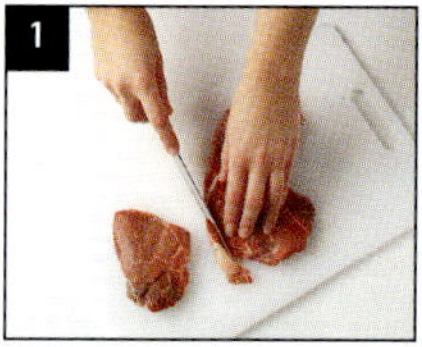

Mediterranean-style Fish Soup

Serves 4 • Calories per serving: 270 • Fat content per serving: 5.3 g

INGREDIENTS

1 tbsp olive oil
1 large onion, chopped
2 garlic cloves, finely chopped
425 ml/15 fl oz/1$^3/_4$ cups fresh fish stock
150 ml/5 fl oz/$^2/_3$ cup dry white wine
1 bay leaf
1 sprig each fresh thyme, rosemary and oregano
450 g/1 lb firm white fish fillets (such as cod, monkfish or halibut), skinned and cut into 2.5 cm/1 inch cubes
450 g/1 lb fresh mussels, prepared
400 g/14 oz can chopped tomatoes
225 g/8 oz peeled prawns (shrimp), thawed if frozen
salt and pepper
sprigs of thyme, to garnish

TO SERVE:
lemon wedges
4 slices toasted French bread, rubbed with cut garlic clove

1 Heat the oil in a large pan and gently fry the onion and garlic for 2–3 minutes until just softened.

2 Pour in the stock and wine and bring to the boil. Tie the bay leaf and herbs together with clean string and add to the saucepan together with the fish and mussels. Stir well, cover and simmer for 5 minutes.

3 Stir in the tomatoes and prawns (shrimp) and continue to cook for a further 3–4 minutes until piping hot and the fish is cooked through.

4 Discard the herbs and any mussels that have not opened. Season and ladle into warm bowls. Garnish with sprigs of thyme and serve with lemon wedges and toasted bread.

COOK'S TIP

Traditionally, the toasted bread is placed at the bottom of the bowl and the soup spooned over the top. For convenience, look out for prepared, cooked shellfish mixtures, which you could use instead of fresh fish. Simply add to the soup with the tomatoes in step 3.

Lentil, Pasta & Vegetable Soup

Serves 4 • CALORIES PER SERVING: 378 • FAT CONTENT PER SERVING: 4.9 G

INGREDIENTS

1 tbsp olive oil
1 medium onion, chopped
4 garlic cloves, finely chopped
350 g/12 oz carrot, sliced
1 stick celery, sliced
225 g/8 oz/1 1/4 cups red lentils
600 ml/1 pint/2 1/2 cups fresh vegetable stock
700 ml/1 1/4 pint/scant 3 cups boiling water
150 g/5 1/2 oz/scant 1 cup pasta
150 ml/5 fl oz/2/3 cup natural low-fat fromage frais (unsweetened yogurt)
salt and pepper
2 tbsp fresh parsley, chopped, to garnish

1 Heat the oil in a large saucepan and gently fry the prepared onion, garlic, carrot and celery, stirring gently, for 5 minutes until the vegetables begin to soften.

2 Add the lentils, stock and boiling water. Season with salt and pepper to taste, stir and bring back to the boil. Simmer, uncovered, for 15 minutes until the lentils are completely tender. Allow to cool for 10 minutes.

3 Meanwhile, bring another saucepan of water to the boil and cook the pasta according to the instructions on the packet. Drain well and set aside.

4 Place the soup in a blender and process until smooth. Return to a saucepan and add the pasta. Bring back to a simmer and heat for 2–3 minutes until piping hot. Remove from the heat and stir in the fromage frais (yogurt). Season if necessary.

5 Serve sprinkled with chopped parsley.

COOK'S TIP

Avoid boiling the soup once the fromage frais (yogurt) has been added. Otherwise it will separate and become watery, spoiling the appearance of the soup.

Tomato & Red (Bell) Pepper Soup

Serves 4 • CALORIES PER SERVING: 93 • FAT CONTENT PER SERVING: 1 G

INGREDIENTS

2 large red (bell) peppers
1 large onion, chopped
2 sticks celery, trimmed and chopped
1 garlic clove, crushed
600 ml/1 pint/$2^1/2$ cups fresh vegetable stock
2 bay leaves
2 x 400 g/14 oz cans plum tomatoes
salt and pepper
2 spring onions (scallions), finely shredded, to garnish
crusty bread, to serve

1 Preheat the grill (broiler) to hot. Halve and deseed the (bell) peppers, arrange them on the grill (broiler) rack and cook, turning occasionally, for 8–10 minutes until softened and charred.

2 Leave to cool slightly, then carefully peel off the charred skin. Reserving a small piece for garnish, chop the (bell) pepper flesh and place in a large saucepan.

3 Mix in the onion, celery and garlic. Add the stock and the bay leaves. Bring to the boil, cover and simmer for 15 minutes. Remove from the heat.

4 Stir in the tomatoes and transfer to a blender. Process for a few seconds until smooth. Return to the saucepan.

5 Season to taste and heat for 3–4 minutes until piping hot. Ladle into warm bowls and garnish with the reserved (bell) pepper cut into strips and the spring onion (scallion). Serve with crusty bread.

COOK'S TIP

If you prefer a coarser, more robust soup, lightly mash the tomatoes with a wooden spoon and omit the blending process in step 4.

Carrot, Apple & Celery Soup

Serves 4 • CALORIES PER SERVING: 150 • FAT CONTENT PER SERVING: 1.4 G

INGREDIENTS

- 900 g/2 lb carrots, finely diced
- 1 medium onion, chopped
- 3 sticks celery, diced
- 1 litre/1$^{3}/_{4}$ pints/1 quart fresh vegetable stock
- 3 medium-sized eating (dessert) apples
- 2 tbsp tomato purée (paste)
- 1 bay leaf
- 2 tsp caster (superfine) sugar
- $^{1}/_{4}$ large lemon
- salt and pepper
- celery leaves, washed and shredded, to garnish

1 Place the carrots, onion and celery in a large saucepan and add the stock. Bring to the boil, cover and simmer for 10 minutes.

2 Meanwhile, peel, core and dice 2 of the eating (dessert) apples. Add the pieces of apple, tomato purée (paste), bay leaf and caster (superfine) sugar to the saucepan and bring to the boil. Reduce the heat, half cover and allow to simmer for 20 minutes. Remove and discard the bay leaf.

3 Meanwhile, wash, core and cut the remaining apple into thin slices, leaving on the skin. Place the apple slices in a small saucepan and squeeze over the lemon juice. Heat gently and simmer for 1–2 minutes until tender. Drain and set aside.

4 Place the carrot and apple mixture in a blender or food processor and blend until smooth. Alternatively, press the carrot and apple mixture through a sieve with the back of a wooden spoon.

5 Gently re-heat the soup if necessary and season with salt and pepper to taste. Ladle the soup into warm bowls and serve topped with the reserved apple slices and shredded celery leaves.

COOK'S TIP

Soaking light coloured fruit in lemon juice helps to prevent it from turning brown.

Parsleyed Chicken & Ham Pâté

Serves 4 • CALORIES PER SERVING: 132 • FAT CONTENT PER SERVING: 1.8 G

INGREDIENTS

225 g/8 oz lean, skinless chicken, cooked
100 g/3 1/2 oz lean ham, trimmed
small bunch fresh parsley
1 tsp lime rind, grated
2 tbsp lime juice
1 garlic clove, peeled
125 ml/4 1/2 fl oz/1/2 cup low-fat natural fromage frais (unsweetened yogurt)
salt and pepper
1 tsp lime zest, to garnish

TO SERVE:
wedges of lime
crisp bread

1 Dice the chicken and ham and place in a blender or food processor. Add the parsley, lime rind and juice, and garlic and process well until finely minced. Alternatively, finely chop the chicken, ham, parsley and garlic and place in a bowl. Mix gently with the lime rind and juice.

2 Transfer the mixture to a bowl and mix in the fromage frais (yogurt). Season with salt and pepper to taste, cover and leave to chill in the refrigerator for about 30 minutes.

3 Transfer the pâté to individual serving dishes and garnish with lime zest.

4 Serve the parsleyed chicken and ham pâtés with lime wedges and crisp bread.

VARIATION

This pâté can be made equally successfully with other kinds of minced, lean, cooked meat such as turkey, beef and pork. Alternatively, replace the chicken and ham with peeled prawns (shrimp) and/or white crab meat or with canned tuna in brine, drained. Remember that removing the skin from poultry reduces the fat content of any dish.

Baked Potatoes with a Spicy Filling

Serves 4 • CALORIES PER SERVING: 354 • FAT CONTENT PER SERVING: 5.9 G

INGREDIENTS

4 baking potatoes, each about 300 g/10½ oz
1 tbsp vegetable oil (optional)
400 g/14 oz can chick-peas (garbanzo beans), drained
1 tsp ground coriander
1 tsp ground cumin
4 tbsp fresh coriander (cilantro), chopped
150 ml/5 fl oz/⅔ cup low-fat natural (unsweetened) yogurt
salt and pepper
salad, to serve

1 Preheat the oven to 200°C/400°F/Gas Mark 6. Scrub the potatoes and pat them dry with absorbent kitchen paper. Prick them all over with a fork, brush with oil (if using) and season.

2 Place the potatoes on a baking sheet (cookie sheet) and bake for 1–1¼ hours or until cooked through. Leave to cool for 10 minutes.

3 Meanwhile, mash the chick-peas (garbanzo beans) with a fork or potato masher. Stir in the spices and half the chopped coriander (cilantro). Cover and set aside.

4 Halve the cooked potatoes and scoop the flesh into a bowl, keeping the shells intact. Mash the flesh until smooth and gently mix into the chick-pea (garbanzo bean) mixture with the yogurt. Season well.

5 Fill the potato shells with the potato and chick-pea (garbanzo bean) mixture. Return the potatoes to the oven and bake for 10–15 minutes until heated through. Serve sprinkled with the remaining chopped coriander (cilantro) and a fresh salad.

COOK'S TIP

For an even lower fat version of this recipe, bake the potatoes without oiling them first.

Pork Stroganoff

Serves 4 • CALORIES PER SERVING: 197 • FAT CONTENT PER SERVING: 7 G

INGREDIENTS

350 g/12 oz lean pork fillet
1 tbsp vegetable oil
1 medium onion, chopped
2 garlic cloves, crushed
25 g/1 oz plain (all-purpose) flour
2 tbsp tomato purée (paste)
425 ml/15 fl oz/1¾ cups fresh chicken or vegetable stock
125 g/4½ oz button mushrooms, sliced
1 large green (bell) pepper, deseeded and diced
½ tsp ground nutmeg
4 tbsp low-fat natural (unsweetened) yogurt, plus extra to serve
salt and pepper
white rice, freshly boiled, to serve
ground nutmeg and chopped parsley, to garnish

1 Trim away any excess fat and silver skin from the pork, then cut the meat into slices about 1 cm/½ inch thick.

2 Heat the oil in a large frying pan (skillet) and gently fry the pork, onion and garlic for 4–5 minutes until lightly browned.

3 Stir in the flour and tomato purée (paste), pour in the stock and stir to mix thoroughly.

4 Add the mushrooms, (bell) pepper, seasoning and nutmeg. Bring to the boil, cover and simmer for 20 minutes or until the pork is tender and cooked through.

5 Remove the saucepan from the heat and stir in the yogurt.

6 Garnish the boiled rice with chopped parsley. Spoon extra yogurt on top of the pork and mushrooms and dust with a little ground nutmeg.

COOK'S TIP

You can buy ready-made meat, vegetable and fish stocks from leading supermarkets. Although more expensive they are better nutritionally than stock cubes which are high in salt and artificial flavourings. However, home-made stock is best of all.

2

4

5

Pork with Ratatouille Sauce

Serves 4 • CALORIES PER SERVING: 214 • FAT CONTENT PER SERVING: 5.6 G

INGREDIENTS

4 lean, boneless pork chops, about 125 g/4 1/2 oz each
1 tsp dried mixed herbs
salt and pepper
baked potatoes, to serve

SAUCE:
1 medium onion
1 garlic clove
1 small green (bell) pepper
1 small yellow (bell) pepper
1 medium courgette (zucchini)
100 g/3 1/2 oz button mushrooms
400 g/14 oz can chopped tomatoes
2 tbsp tomato purée (paste)
1 tsp dried mixed herbs
1 tsp caster (superfine) sugar

1 To make the sauce, peel and chop the onion and garlic. Deseed and dice the (bell) peppers. Trim and dice the courgette (zucchini). Wipe and halve the mushrooms.

2 Place all of the vegetables in a saucepan and stir in the chopped tomatoes and tomato purée (paste). Add the dried herbs, sugar and plenty of seasoning. Bring to the boil, cover and simmer for 20 minutes.

3 Meanwhile, preheat the grill (broiler) to medium. Trim away any excess fat from the chops, then season on both sides and rub in the dried mixed herbs. Cook the chops for 5 minutes, then turn over and cook for a further 6–7 minutes or until cooked through.

4 Drain the chops on absorbent kitchen paper and serve accompanied with the sauce and baked potatoes.

COOK'S TIP

This vegetable sauce could be served with any other grilled (broiled) or baked meat or fish. It would also make an excellent alternative filling for Savoury Crêpes.

Pan-seared Beef with Ginger, Pineapple & Chilli

Serves 4 • CALORIES PER SERVING: 191 • FAT CONTENT PER SERVING: 5.1 G

INGREDIENTS

4 lean beef steaks (such as rump, sirloin or fillet), 100 g/3 1/2 oz each
2 tbsp ginger wine
2.5 cm/1 inch piece root (fresh) ginger, finely chopped
1 garlic clove, crushed
1 tsp ground chilli
1 tsp vegetable oil
salt and pepper
red chilli strips, to garnish

TO SERVE:
freshly cooked noodles
2 spring onions (scallions), shredded

RELISH:
225 g/8 oz fresh pineapple
1 small red (bell) pepper
1 red chilli
2 tbsp light soy sauce
1 piece stem ginger in syrup, drained and chopped

1 Trim any excess fat from the beef. Using a meat mallet or covered rolling pin, pound the steaks until 1 cm/½ inch thick. Season on both sides and place in a shallow dish.

2 Mix the ginger wine, root (fresh) ginger, garlic and chilli and pour over the meat. Cover and chill for 30 minutes.

3 To make the relish, peel and finely chop the pineapple and place it in a bowl. Halve, deseed and finely chop the (bell) pepper and chilli. Stir into the pineapple together with the soy sauce and stem ginger. Cover and chill.

4 Brush a grill (broiler) pan with the oil and heat until hot. Drain the beef and add to the pan, pressing down to seal. Lower the heat and cook for 5 minutes. Turn the steaks over and cook for 5 minutes.

5 Drain the steaks on kitchen paper and transfer to serving plates. Garnish with chilli strips, and serve with noodles, spring onions (scallions) and the relish.

Beef & Tomato Gratin

Serves 4 • CALORIES PER SERVING: 319 • FAT CONTENT PER SERVING: 10.3 G

INGREDIENTS

- 350 g/12 oz lean beef, minced (ground)
- 1 large onion, finely chopped
- 1 tsp dried mixed herbs
- 1 tbsp plain (all-purpose) flour
- 300 ml/$^1/_2$ pint/1$^1/_4$ cups beef stock
- 1 tbsp tomato purée (paste)
- 2 large tomatoes, thinly sliced
- 4 medium courgettes (zucchini), thinly sliced
- 2 tbsp cornflour (cornstarch)
- 300 ml/$^1/_2$ pint/1$^1/_4$ cups skimmed milk
- 150 ml/5 fl oz/$^2/_3$ cup low-fat natural fromage frais (unsweetened yogurt)
- 1 medium egg yolk
- 4 tbsp Parmesan cheese, freshly grated
- salt and pepper

1 Preheat the oven to 190°C/375°F/Gas Mark 5. In a large pan, dry-fry the beef and onion for 4–5 minutes until browned.

2 Stir in the herbs, flour, stock and tomato purée (paste), and season. Bring to the boil and simmer for 30 minutes until thickened.

3 Transfer the beef mixture to an ovenproof gratin dish. Cover with a layer of the sliced tomatoes and then add a layer of sliced courgettes (zucchini). Set aside until required.

4 Blend the cornflour (cornstarch) with a little milk in a small bowl. Pour the remaining milk into a saucepan and bring to the boil. Add the cornflour (cornstarch) mixture and cook, stirring, for 1–2 minutes until thickened. Remove from the heat and beat in the fromage frais (yogurt) and egg yolk. Season well.

5 Place the dish on to a baking sheet (cookie sheet) and spread the white sauce over the layer of courgettes (zucchini). Sprinkle with grated Parmesan and bake in the oven for 25–30 minutes until golden-brown. Serve immediately.

Venison & Garlic Mash

Serves 4 • CALORIES PER SERVING: 503 • FAT CONTENT PER SERVING: 6.1 G

INGREDIENTS

8 medallions of venison, 75 g/2$^3/_4$ oz each
1 tbsp vegetable oil
1 red onion, chopped
150 ml/5 fl oz/$^2/_3$ cup fresh beef stock
150 ml/5 fl oz/$^2/_3$ cup red wine
3 tbsp redcurrant jelly
100 g/3$^1/_2$ oz no-need-to-soak dried, pitted prunes
2 tsp cornflour (cornstarch)
2 tbsp brandy
salt and pepper
patty pans, to serve (optional)

GARLIC MASH:
900 g/2 lb potatoes, peeled and diced
$^1/_2$ tsp garlic purée (paste)
2 tbsp low-fat natural fromage frais (unsweetened yogurt)
4 tbsp fresh parsley, chopped

1 Trim off any excess fat from the meat and season with salt and pepper on both sides.

2 Heat the oil in a pan and fry the medallions with the onions on a high heat for 2 minutes on each side until brown.

3 Lower the heat and pour in the stock and wine. Add the redcurrant jelly and prunes and stir until the jelly melts. Bring to the boil, cover and simmer for 10 minutes until cooked through.

4 Meanwhile, make the garlic mash. Place the potatoes in a saucepan and cover with water. Bring to the boil and cook for 8–10 minutes until tender. Drain.

5 Mash the potatoes until smooth. Add the garlic purée (paste), fromage frais (yogurt) and parsley and blend thoroughly. Season, set aside and keep warm.

6 Remove the medallions from the pan with a slotted spoon and keep warm.

7 Blend the cornflour (cornstarch) with the brandy in a small bowl and add to the pan juices. Heat, stirring, until thickened. Season to taste. Serve the venison with the sauce and garlic mash.

Venison Meatballs with Sherried Kumquat Sauce

Serves 4 • CALORIES PER SERVING: 178 • FAT CONTENT PER SERVING: 2.1 G

INGREDIENTS

450 g/1 lb lean venison, minced (ground)
1 small leek, finely chopped
1 medium carrot, finely grated
1/2 tsp ground nutmeg
1 medium egg white, lightly beaten
salt and pepper

TO SERVE:
freshly cooked pasta or noodles
freshly cooked vegetables

SAUCE:
100 g/3 1/2 oz kumquats
15 g/1/2 oz caster (superfine) sugar
150 ml/5 fl oz/2/3 cup water
4 tbsp dry sherry
1 tsp cornflour (cornstarch)

1 Place the venison in a mixing bowl together with the leek, carrot, seasoning and nutmeg. Add the egg white and bind the ingredients together with your hands until the mixture is well moulded and firm.

2 Divide the mixture into 16 equal portions. Using your fingers, form each portion into a small round ball.

3 Bring a large saucepan of water to the boil. Arrange the meatballs on a layer of baking parchment in a steamer or large sieve (strainer) and place over the boiling water. Cover and steam for 10 minutes until cooked through.

4 Meanwhile, make the sauce. Wash and thinly slice the kumquats. Place them in a saucepan with the sugar and water and bring to the boil. Simmer for 2–3 minutes until just tender.

5 Blend the sherry and cornflour (cornstarch) together and add to the pan. Heat through, stirring, until the sauce thickens. Season to taste.

6 Drain the meatballs and transfer to a serving plate. Spoon over the sauce and serve.

2

3

5

Lamb, (Bell) Pepper, & Couscous

Serves 4 • CALORIES PER SERVING: 522 • FAT CONTENT PER SERVING: 12.5 G

INGREDIENTS

- 2 medium red onions, sliced
- juice of 1 lemon
- 1 large red (bell) pepper, deseeded and thickly sliced
- 1 large green (bell) pepper, deseeded and thickly sliced
- 1 large orange (bell) pepper, deseeded and thickly sliced
- pinch of saffron strands
- cinnamon stick, broken
- 1 tbsp clear honey
- 300 ml/½ pint/1¼ cups vegetable stock
- 2 tsp olive oil
- 350 g/12 oz lean lamb fillet, trimmed and sliced
- 1 tsp Harissa paste
- 200 g/7 oz can chopped tomatoes
- 425 g/15 oz can chick-peas (garbanzo beans), drained
- 350 g/12 oz precooked couscous
- 2 tsp ground cinnamon
- salt and pepper

1 Toss the onions in the lemon juice and transfer to a saucepan. Mix in the (bell) peppers, saffron, cinnamon stick and honey. Pour in the stock, bring to the boil, cover and simmer for 5 minutes.

2 Meanwhile, heat the oil in a frying pan (skillet) and gently fry the lamb for 3–4 minutes until browned all over.

3 Using a slotted spoon, drain the lamb and transfer it to the pan with the onions and peppers. Season and stir in the Harissa paste, tomatoes and chick-peas (garbanzo beans). Mix well, bring back to the boil and simmer, uncovered, for 20 minutes.

4 Meanwhile, soak the couscous, following the instructions on the packet. Bring a saucepan of water to the boil. Transfer the couscous to a steamer or sieve (strainer) lined with muslin (cheesecloth) and place over the pan of boiling water. Cover and steam as directed.

5 Transfer the couscous to a warm serving platter and dust with ground cinnamon. Remove and discard the cinnamon stick. Spoon the stew over the couscous to serve.

1

3

4

Hot Pot Chops

Serves 4 • CALORIES PER SERVING: 252 • FAT CONTENT PER SERVING: 11.3 G

INGREDIENTS

- 4 lean, boneless lamb leg steaks, about 125 g/4 1/2 oz each
- 1 small onion, thinly sliced
- 1 medium carrot, thinly sliced
- 1 medium potato, thinly sliced
- 1 tsp olive oil
- 1 tsp dried rosemary
- salt and pepper
- fresh rosemary, to garnish
- freshly steamed green vegetables, to serve

1 Preheat the oven to 180°C/350°F/Gas Mark 4. Using a sharp knife, trim any excess fat from the lamb steaks.

2 Season both sides of the steaks with salt and pepper to taste and arrange them on a baking sheet (cookie sheet).

3 Alternate layers of sliced onion, carrot and potato on top of each lamb steak.

4 Brush the tops of the potato lightly with oil, season well with salt and pepper to taste and then sprinkle with a little dried rosemary.

5 Bake the hot pot chops in the oven for 25–30 minutes until the lamb is tender and cooked through.

6 Drain the lamb on absorbent kitchen paper and transfer to a warmed serving plate. Garnish with fresh rosemary and serve accompanied with a selection of green vegetables.

VARIATION

This recipe would work equally well with boneless chicken breasts. Pound the chicken slightly with a meat mallet or covered rolling pin so that the pieces are the same thickness throughout.

Minty Lamb Burgers

Serves 4 • CALORIES PER SERVING: 237 • FAT CONTENT PER SERVING: 7.8 G

INGREDIENTS

350 g/12 oz lean lamb, minced (ground)
1 medium onion, finely chopped
4 tbsp dry wholemeal breadcrumbs
2 tbsp mint jelly
salt and pepper

TO SERVE:
4 wholemeal baps, split
2 large tomatoes, sliced
small piece of cucumber, sliced
lettuce leaves

RELISH:
4 tbsp low-fat natural fromage frais (unsweetened yogurt)
1 tbsp mint jelly, softened
5 cm/2 inch piece of cucumber, finely diced
1 tbsp fresh mint, chopped

1 Place the lamb in a large bowl and mix in the onion, breadcrumbs and jelly. Season well, then mould the ingredients together with your hands to form a firm mixture.

2 Divide the mixture into 4 and shape each portion into a round measuring 10 cm/4 inches across. Place the rounds on a plate lined with baking parchment and leave to chill for 30 minutes.

3 Preheat the grill (broiler) to medium. Line a grill (broiler) rack with baking parchment, securing the ends under the rack, and place the burgers on top. Cook for 8 minutes, then turn over the burgers and cook for a further 7 minutes or until cooked through.

4 Meanwhile, make the relish. Mix together the fromage frais (unsweetened yogurt), mint jelly, cucumber and freshly chopped mint in a bowl. Cover and leave to chill in the refrigerator until required.

5 Drain the burgers on absorbent kitchen paper. Serve the burgers inside the baps with sliced tomatoes, cucumber, lettuce and relish.

1

3

4

Chicken Pasta Bake with Fennel & Raisins

Serves 4 • CALORIES PER SERVING: 521 • FAT CONTENT PER SERVING: 15.5 G

INGREDIENTS

2 bulbs fennel
2 medium red onions, shredded
1 tbsp lemon juice
125 g/4½ oz button mushrooms
1 tbsp olive oil
225 g/8 oz penne (quills)
60 g/2 oz/⅓ cup raisins
225 g/8 oz lean, boneless cooked chicken, skinned and shredded
375 g/13 oz low-fat soft cheese with garlic and herbs
125 g/4½ oz low-fat Mozzarella cheese, thinly sliced
2 tbsp Parmesan cheese, grated
salt and pepper

1 Preheat the oven to 200°C/400°F/Gas Mark 6. Trim the fennel, reserving the green fronds for garnishing, and slice the bulbs thinly. Coat the onions in the lemon juice. Quarter the mushrooms.

2 Heat the oil in a large frying pan (skillet) and fry the fennel, onion and mushrooms for 4–5 minutes, stirring, until just softened. Season and transfer the vegetable mixture to a large bowl.

3 Bring a pan of lightly salted water to the boil and cook the penne (quills) according to the instructions on the packet until 'al dente' (just cooked). Drain and mix the pasta with the vegetables.

4 Stir the raisins and chicken into the pasta mixture. Soften the soft cheese by beating it, then mix into the pasta and chicken – the heat from the pasta should make the cheese melt slightly.

5 Put the mixture into an ovenproof dish and transfer to a baking sheet (cookie sheet). Arrange the Mozzarella on top and sprinkle with the Parmesan. Bake for 20–25 minutes until golden. Garnish with fennel fronds and serve.

Baked Southern-style Chicken & Chips

Serves 4 • CALORIES PER SERVING: 402 • FAT CONTENT PER SERVING: 7.4 G

INGREDIENTS

4 baking potatoes, each 225 g/8 oz
1 tbsp sunflower oil
2 tsp coarse sea salt
2 tbsp plain (all-purpose) flour
pinch of cayenne pepper
$\frac{1}{2}$ tsp paprika pepper
$\frac{1}{2}$ tsp dried thyme
8 chicken drumsticks, skin removed
1 medium egg, beaten
2 tbsp cold water
6 tbsp dry white breadcrumbs
salt and pepper

TO SERVE:
low-fat coleslaw salad
sweetcorn relish

1 Preheat the oven to 200°C/400°F/Gas Mark 6. Wash and scrub the potatoes and cut each into 8 equal portions. Place in a clean plastic bag and add the oil. Seal and shake well to coat.

2 Arrange the potato wedges, skin side down, on a non-stick baking sheet (cookie sheet), sprinkle over the sea salt and bake in the oven for 30–35 minutes until they are tender and golden-brown.

3 Meanwhile, mix the flour, cayenne, paprika, thyme and salt and pepper to taste together on a plate. Press the chicken drumsticks into the seasoned flour to lightly coat all over.

4 On one plate mix together the egg and water. On another plate sprinkle the breadcrumbs. Dip the chicken drumsticks first in the egg and then in the breadcrumbs. Place on a non-stick baking sheet (cookie sheet).

5 Bake the chicken drumsticks alongside the potato wedges for 30 minutes, turning after 15 minutes, until they are tender and cooked through.

6 Drain the potato wedges thoroughly on absorbent kitchen paper to remove any excess fat. Serve the potato wedges with the chicken, accompanied by low-fat coleslaw and sweetcorn relish, if wished.

Sage Chicken & Rice

Serves 4 • CALORIES PER SERVING: 391 • FAT CONTENT PER SERVING: 3.9 G

INGREDIENTS

1 large onion, chopped
1 garlic clove, crushed
2 sticks celery, sliced
2 carrots, diced
2 sprigs fresh sage
300 ml/$^1/_2$ pint/1$^1/_4$ cups chicken stock
350 g/12 oz boneless, skinless chicken breasts
225 g/8 oz/1$^1/_3$ cups mixed brown and wild rice
400 g/14 oz can chopped tomatoes
dash of Tabasco sauce
2 medium courgettes (zucchini), trimmed and thinly sliced
100 g/3$^1/_2$ oz lean ham, diced
salt and pepper
fresh sage, to garnish

TO SERVE:
salad leaves
crusty bread

1 Place the onion, garlic, celery, carrots and sprigs of fresh sage in a large saucepan and pour in the chicken stock. Bring to the boil, cover the pan and simmer for 5 minutes.

2 Cut the chicken into 2.5 cm/1 inch cubes and stir into the pan with the vegetables. Cover the pan and continue to cook for a further 5 minutes.

3 Stir in the rice and chopped tomatoes. Add a dash of Tabasco sauce to taste and season well. Bring to the boil, cover and simmer for 25 minutes.

4 Stir in the sliced courgettes (zucchini) and diced ham and continue to cook, uncovered, for a further 10 minutes, stirring occasionally, until the rice is just tender.

5 Remove and discard the sprigs of sage. Garnish with a few sage leaves and serve with a fresh salad and fresh crusty bread.

COOK'S TIP

If you do not have fresh sage, use 1 tsp of dried sage in step 1.

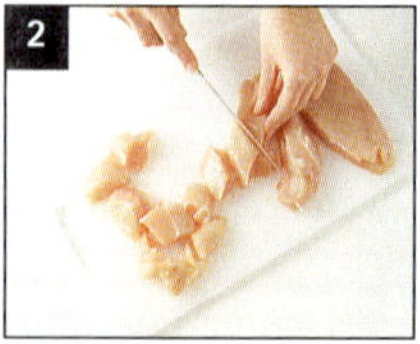

Crispy-Topped Stuffed Chicken

Serves 4 • Calories per serving: 211 • Fat content per serving: 3.8 g

INGREDIENTS

4 boneless chicken breasts, about150 g/5$^1/_2$ oz each, skinned
4 sprigs fresh tarragon
$^1/_2$ small orange (bell) pepper, deseeded and sliced
1$^1/_2$ small green (bell) pepper, deseeded and sliced
15 g/$^1/_2$ oz wholemeal breadcrumbs
1 tbsp sesame seeds
4 tbsp lemon juice
1 small red (bell) pepper, halved and deseeded
200 g/7 oz can chopped tomatoes
1 small red chilli, deseeded and chopped
$^1/_4$ tsp celery salt
salt and pepper
fresh tarragon, to garnish

1 Preheat the oven to 200°C/400°F/Gas Mark 6. Slit the chicken breasts with a sharp knife to create a pocket in each. Season inside each pocket.

2 Place a sprig of tarragon and a few slices of orange and green (bell) peppers in each pocket. Place the chicken breasts on a baking sheet (cookie sheet) and sprinkle over the breadcrumbs and sesame seeds.

3 Spoon 1 tbsp lemon juice over each chicken breast and bake in the oven for 35–40 minutes until the chicken is cooked through.

4 Preheat the grill (broiler) to hot. Arrange the red (bell) pepper halves, skin side up, on the rack and cook for 5–6 minutes until the skin blisters. Cool for 10 minutes; peel off the skins.

5 Put the red (bell) pepper in a blender, add the tomatoes, chilli and celery salt and process for a few seconds. Season to taste. Alternatively, finely chop the red (bell) pepper and press through a sieve with the tomatoes and chilli.

6 When the chicken is cooked, heat the sauce, spoon a little on to a warm plate and arrange a chicken breast in the centre. Garnish with tarragon and serve.

1

3

5

Chicken & Plum Casserole

Serves 4 • CALORIES PER SERVING: 285 • FAT CONTENT PER SERVING: 6.4 G

INGREDIENTS

- 2 rashers lean back bacon, rinds removed, trimmed and chopped
- 1 tbsp sunflower oil
- 450 g/1 lb skinless, boneless chicken thighs, cut into 4 equal strips
- 1 garlic clove, crushed
- 175 g/6 oz shallots, halved
- 225 g/8 oz plums, halved or quartered (if large) and stoned
- 1 tbsp light muscovado sugar
- 150 ml/5 fl oz/$^{2}/_{3}$ cup dry sherry
- 2 tbsp plum sauce
- 450 ml/16 fl oz/2 cups fresh chicken stock
- 2 tsp cornflour (cornstarch) mixed with 4 tsp cold water
- 2 tbsp flat-leaf parsley, chopped, to garnish
- crusty bread, to serve

1 In a large, non-stick frying pan (skillet), dry fry the bacon for 2–3 minutes until the juices run out. Remove the bacon from the pan with a slotted spoon, set aside and keep warm until required.

2 In the same frying pan (skillet), heat the oil and fry the chicken with the garlic and shallots for 4–5 minutes, stirring occasionally, until well browned all over.

3 Return the bacon to the frying pan (skillet) and stir in the plums, sugar, sherry, plum sauce and stock. Bring to the boil and simmer for 20 minutes until the plums have softened and the chicken is cooked through.

4 Add the cornflour (cornstarch) mixture to the frying pan (skillet) and cook, stirring, for a further 2–3 minutes until thickened.

5 Spoon the casserole on to warm serving plates and garnish with chopped parsley. Serve with chunks of bread to mop up the fruity gravy.

VARIATION

Chunks of lean turkey or pork would also go well with this combination of flavours. The cooking time will remain the same.

Curried Turkey with Apricots & Sultanas

Serves 4 • CALORIES PER SERVING: 418 • FAT CONTENT PER SERVING: 7.9 G

INGREDIENTS

- 1 tbsp vegetable oil
- 1 large onion, chopped
- 450 g/1 lb skinless turkey breast, cut into cubes
- 3 tbsp mild curry paste
- 300 ml/½ pint/1¼ cups fresh chicken stock
- 175 g/6 oz frozen peas
- 400 g/14 oz can apricot halves in natural juice
- 50 g/1¾ oz/⅓ cup sultanas (golden raisins)
- 350 g/12 oz/6 cups basmati rice, freshly cooked
- 1 tsp ground coriander
- 4 tbsp fresh coriander (cilantro), chopped
- 1 green chilli, deseeded and sliced
- salt and pepper

1 Heat the oil in a large saucepan and fry the onion and turkey for 4–5 minutes until the onion has softened and the turkey is a light golden colour.

2 Stir in the curry paste. Pour in the stock, stirring, and bring to the boil. Cover and simmer for 15 minutes. Stir in the peas and bring back to the boil. Cover and simmer for about 5 minutes.

3 Drain the apricots, reserving the juice, and cut into thick slices. Add to the curry, stirring in a little of the juice if the mixture is becoming dry. Add the sultanas (golden raisins) and cook for 2 minutes.

4 Mix the rice with the ground coriander and fresh coriander (cilantro), stir in the chilli and season with salt and pepper to taste. Transfer the rice to warm plates and top with the turkey curry.

VARIATION

Peaches can be used instead of the apricots if you prefer. Cook in exactly the same way.

Duck with Kiwi Fruit & Raspberries

Serves 4 • CALORIES PER SERVING: 286 • FAT CONTENT PER SERVING: 8.4 G

INGREDIENTS

450 g/1 lb boneless duck breasts, skin removed
2 tbsp raspberry vinegar
2 tbsp brandy
1 tbsp clear honey
1 tsp sunflower oil
2 kiwi fruit, peeled and sliced thinly
salt and pepper

SAUCE:
225 g/8 oz raspberries, thawed if frozen
300 ml/½ pint/1¼ cups rosé wine
2 tsp cornflour (cornstarch) blended with 4 tsp cold water

1 Preheat the grill (broiler) to medium. Skin and trim the duck breasts to remove any excess fat. Score the flesh in diagonal lines and pound it with a meat mallet or a covered rolling pin until it is 1.5 cm/¾ inch thick.

2 Place the duck breasts in a shallow dish. Mix together the vinegar, brandy and honey in a small bowl and spoon over the duck. Cover and leave to chill for about 1 hour.

3 Drain the duck, reserving the marinade, and place on the grill (broiler) rack. Season and brush with oil. Cook for 10 minutes, turn over, season and brush with oil again. Cook for 8–10 minutes until the meat is cooked through.

4 For the sauce, reserve 60 g/2 oz raspberries and place the rest in a pan. Add the reserved marinade and the wine. Bring to the boil and simmer for 5 minutes until slightly reduced.

5 Strain the sauce through a sieve, pressing the raspberries with the back of a spoon. Return the liquid to the pan and add the cornflour (cornstarch) paste. Heat through, stirring, until thickened. Add the reserved raspberries and season.

6 Slice the duck breast and arrange fanned out on warm serving plates, alternating with slices of kiwi fruit. Spoon over the sauce and serve.

1

2

4

Fish Cakes with Piquant Tomato Sauce

Serves 4 • CALORIES PER SERVING: 320 • FAT CONTENT PER SERVING: 7.5 G

INGREDIENTS

450 g/1 lb potatoes, diced
225 g/8 oz haddock fillet
225 g/8 oz trout fillet
1 bay leaf
425 ml/15 fl oz/1 3/4 cups fresh fish stock
2 tbsp low-fat natural fromage frais (unsweetened yogurt)
4 tbsp fresh snipped chives
75 g/2 3/4 oz dry white breadcrumbs
1 tbsp sunflower oil
salt and pepper
freshly snipped chives, to garnish
lemon wedges and salad leaves, to serve

PIQUANT TOMATO SAUCE:
200 ml/7 fl oz/3/4 cup passata (sieved tomatoes)
4 tbsp dry white wine
4 tbsp low-fat natural (unsweetened) yogurt
chilli powder

1 Place the potatoes in a pan and cover with water. Bring to the boil and cook for 10 minutes until tender. Drain and mash.

2 Place the fish in a pan with the bay leaf and stock. Bring to the boil and simmer for 7–8 minutes. Remove the fish and flake the flesh away from the skin.

3 Mix the fish with the potato, fromage frais (yogurt), chives and seasoning. Cool, then cover and chill for 1 hour.

4 Sprinkle the breadcrumbs on to a plate. Divide the fish mixture into 8 and form each portion into a patty, about 7.5 cm/3 inches in diameter. Press each fish cake into the breadcrumbs.

5 Brush a frying pan (skillet) with oil and fry the fish cakes for 6 minutes. Turn the fish cakes over and cook for a further 5–6 minutes until golden. Drain on kitchen paper and keep warm.

6 To make the sauce, heat the passata (sieved tomatoes) and wine. Season, remove from the heat and stir in the yogurt. Return to the heat, sprinkle with chilli powder and serve with the fish cakes.

3

4

5

Provençal-style Mussels

Serves 4 • CALORIES PER SERVING: 185 • FAT CONTENT PER SERVING: 6.5 G

INGREDIENTS

1 tbsp olive oil
1 large onion, finely chopped
1 garlic clove, finely chopped
1 small red (bell) pepper, deseeded and finely chopped
sprig of rosemary
2 bay leaves
400 g/14 oz can chopped tomatoes
150 ml/5 fl oz/$^{2}/_{3}$ cup white wine
1 courgette (zucchini), diced finely
2 tbsp tomato purée (paste)
1 tsp caster (superfine) sugar
50 g/1$^{3}/_{4}$ oz pitted black olives in brine, drained and chopped
675 g/1$^{1}/_{2}$ lb cooked New Zealand mussels in their shells
1 tsp orange rind
salt and pepper
2 tbsp chopped, fresh parsley, to garnish
crusty bread, to serve

1 Heat the oil in a large saucepan and gently fry the onion, garlic and (bell) pepper for 3–4 minutes until just softened.

2 Add the sprig of rosemary and the bay leaves to the saucepan with the tomatoes and 100 ml/ 3½ fl oz/⅓ cup wine. Season to taste, then bring to the boil and simmer for 15 minutes.

3 Stir in the courgette (zucchini), tomato purée (paste), sugar and olives. Simmer for about 10 minutes.

4 Meanwhile, bring a pan of water to the boil. Arrange the mussels in a steamer or a large sieve (strainer) and place over the water. Sprinkle with the remaining wine and the orange rind. Cover and steam until the mussels open (discard any that remain closed).

5 Remove the mussels with a slotted spoon and arrange on a warm serving plate. Discard the herbs and spoon the sauce over the mussels. Garnish with chopped fresh parsley and serve with fresh, crusty bread.

Citrus Fish Kebabs (Kabobs)

Serves 4 • CALORIES PER SERVING: 335 • FAT CONTENT PER SERVING: 14.5 G

INGREDIENTS

450 g/1 lb firm white fish fillets (such as cod or monkfish)
450 g/1 lb thick salmon fillet
2 large oranges
1 pink grapefruit
1 bunch fresh bay leaves
1 tsp finely grated lemon rind
3 tbsp lemon juice
2 tsp clear honey
2 garlic cloves, crushed
salt and pepper

TO SERVE:
crusty bread
mixed salad

1 Skin the white fish and the salmon, rinse and pat dry on absorbent kitchen paper. Cut each fillet into 16 pieces.

2 Using a sharp knife, remove the skin and pith from the oranges and grapefruit. Cut out the segments of flesh, removing all remaining traces of the pith and dividing membrane.

3 Thread the pieces of fish alternately with the orange and grapefruit segments and the bay leaves on to 8 skewers. Place the kebabs (kabobs) in a shallow dish.

4 Mix together the lemon rind and juice, the honey and garlic. Pour over the fish kebabs (kabobs) and season well. Cover and chill for 2 hours, turning occasionally.

5 Preheat the grill (broiler) to medium. Remove the skewers from the marinade and place on the rack. Cook for 7–8 minutes, turning once, until cooked through.

6 Drain, transfer to serving plates and serve with crusty bread and a fresh salad.

VARIATION

This dish makes an unusual starter. Try it with any firm fish – swordfish or shark, for example – or with tuna for a meatier texture.

Five-spice Salmon with Ginger Stir-fry

Serves 4 • CALORIES PER SERVING: 295 • FAT CONTENT PER SERVING: 18 G

INGREDIENTS

4 salmon fillets, skinned, 115 g/4 oz each
2 tsp five-spice powder
1 large leek
1 large carrot
115 g/4 oz mangetout (snow peas)
2.5 cm/1 inch piece root (fresh) ginger
2 tbsp ginger wine
2 tbsp light soy sauce
1 tbsp vegetable oil
salt and pepper
freshly boiled noodles, to serve

TO GARNISH:
shredded leek
shredded root (fresh) ginger
shredded carrot

1 Wash the salmon and pat dry on absorbent kitchen paper. Rub the five-spice powder into both sides of the fish and season with salt and pepper. Set aside until required.

2 Trim the leek, slice it down the centre and rinse under cold water to remove any dirt. Finely shred the leek. Peel the carrot and cut it into very thin strips. Top and tail the mangetout (snow peas) and cut them into shreds. Peel the ginger and slice thinly into strips.

3 Place all of the vegetables into a large bowl and toss in the ginger wine and 1 tablespoon of soy sauce. Set aside.

4 Preheat the grill (broiler) to medium. Place the salmon fillets on the rack and brush with the remaining soy sauce. Cook for 2–3 minutes on each side until cooked through.

5 While the salmon is cooking, heat the oil in a non-stick wok or large frying pan (skillet) and stir-fry the vegetables for 5 minutes until just tender. Take care that you do not overcook the vegetables – they should still have bite. Transfer to serving plates.

6 Drain the salmon on kitchen paper and serve on a bed of stir-fried vegetables. Garnish with shredded leek, ginger and carrot and serve.

Rice-stuffed Mushrooms

Serves 4 • Calories per serving: 315 • Fat content per serving: 6 g

INGREDIENTS

4 large flat mushrooms
100 g/3 1/2 oz assorted wild mushrooms, sliced
4 dry-pack, sun-dried tomatoes, shredded
150 ml/5 fl oz/2/3 cup dry red wine
4 spring onions (scallions), trimmed and finely chopped
75 g/2 3/4 oz/1 1/2 cups cooked red rice
2 tbsp freshly grated Parmesan cheese
4 thick slices granary bread
salt and pepper
spring onion (scallion), shredded, to garnish

1 Preheat the oven to 190°C/375°F/Gas Mark 5. Peel the flat mushrooms, pull out the stalks and set aside. Finely chop the stalks and place in a saucepan.

2 Add the wild mushrooms to the pan with the tomatoes and red wine. Bring to the boil, cover and simmer gently for 2–3 minutes until just tender. Drain, reserving the cooking liquid, and place in a small bowl.

3 Stir in the spring onions (scallions) and cooked rice. Season well and spoon into the flat mushrooms, pressing the mixture down gently. Sprinkle with the grated Parmesan cheese.

4 Arrange the mushrooms in an ovenproof baking dish and pour the reserved cooking juices around them. Bake in the oven for 20–25 minutes until they are just cooked.

5 Meanwhile, preheat the grill (broiler) to hot. Trim the crusts from the bread and toast on each side until lightly browned.

6 Drain the mushrooms and place each one on to a piece of toasted bread. Garnish with spring onions (scallions) and serve.

Soft Pancakes with Stir-fried Vegetables & Tofu (Bean Curd)

Serves 4 • CALORIES PER SERVING: 215 • FAT CONTENT PER SERVING: 8.5 G

INGREDIENTS

- 1 tbsp vegetable oil
- 1 garlic clove, crushed
- 2.5 cm/1 inch piece root (fresh) ginger, grated
- 1 bunch spring onions (scallions), trimmed and shredded lengthwise
- 100 g/3½ oz mangetout (snow peas), topped, tailed and shredded
- 225 g/8 oz tofu (bean curd), drained and cut into 1 cm/½ inch pieces
- 2 tbsp dark soy sauce, plus extra to serve
- 2 tbsp hoi-sin sauce, plus extra to serve
- 60 g/2 oz canned bamboo shoots, drained
- 60 g/2 oz canned water chestnuts, drained and sliced
- 100 g/3½ oz bean sprouts
- 1 small red chilli, deseeded and sliced thinly
- 1 small bunch fresh chives
- 12 soft Chinese pancakes

TO SERVE:

- shredded Chinese leaves
- 1 cucumber, sliced
- strips of red chilli

1 Heat the oil in a non-stick wok or a large frying pan (skillet) and stir-fry the garlic and ginger for 1 minute. Add the spring onions (scallions), mangetout (snow peas), tofu (bean curd), soy and hoi-sin sauces. Stir-fry for 2 minutes.

2 Add the bamboo shoots, water chestnuts, bean sprouts and red chilli to the pan. Stir-fry for 2 minutes until the vegetables are tender but still have bite. Snip the chives into 2.5 cm/1 inch lengths and stir them into the mixture in the pan.

3 Heat the pancakes according to the instructions on the packet and keep warm.

4 Divide the vegetables and tofu (bean curd) among the pancakes. Roll up the pancakes and serve with the Chinese leaves.

Cheese Hearts with Strawberry Sauce

Serves 4 • CALORIES PER SERVING: 120 • FAT CONTENT PER SERVING: 0.6 G

INGREDIENTS

150 g/5 1/2 oz low-fat cottage cheese
150 ml/5 fl oz/2/3 cup low-fat natural fromage frais (unsweetened yogurt)
1 medium egg white
2 tbsp caster (superfine) sugar
1–2 tsp vanilla essence (extract)
rose-scented geranium leaves, to decorate (optional)

SAUCE:
225 g/8 oz strawberries
4 tbsp unsweetened orange juice
2–3 tsp icing (confectioner's) sugar

1 Line 4 heart-shaped moulds (molds) with clean muslin (cheesecloth). Place a sieve (strainer) over a mixing bowl and using the back of a metal spoon, press through the cottage cheese. Mix in the fromage frais (yogurt).

2 Whisk the egg white until stiff. Fold into the cheeses, with the caster (superfine) sugar and vanilla essence (extract).

3 Place the moulds (molds) on a wire rack set over a roasting tin (pan). Spoon the the cheese mixture into the moulds (molds) and smooth over the tops. Leave to chill for 1 hour or until firm and well drained.

4 To make the sauce, wash the strawberries under cold running water. Reserving a few strawberries for decoration, hull and chop the remainder. Place the strawberries in a blender or food processor with the orange juice and process until smooth. Alternatively, push through a sieve (strainer) to purée. Mix with the icing (confectioner's) sugar to taste. Cover and leave to chill until required.

5 Remove the cheese hearts from the moulds (molds) and transfer to serving plates. Remove the muslin (cheesecloth), decorate with the reserved strawberries and geranium leaves (if using) and serve with the sauce.

Baked Pears with Cinnamon & Brown Sugar

Serves 4 • CALORIES PER SERVING: 160 • FAT CONTENT PER SERVING: 6 G

INGREDIENTS

4 ripe pears
2 tbsp lemon juice
4 tbsp light muscovado sugar
1 tsp ground cinnamon
60 g/2 oz low-fat spread
low-fat custard, to serve
lemon rind, finely grated, to decorate

1 Preheat the oven to 200°C/400°F/Gas Mark 6. Core and peel the pears, then slice them in half lengthwise and brush all over with the lemon juice to prevent the pears from discoloring. Place the pears, cored side down, in a small non-stick roasting tin (pan).

2 Place the sugar, cinnamon and low-fat spread in a small saucepan and heat gently, stirring, until the sugar has melted. Keep the heat low to stop too much water evaporating from the low-fat spread as it gets hot. Spoon the mixture over the pears.

3 Bake for 20–25 minutes or until the pears are tender and golden, occasionally spooning the sugar mixture over the fruit during the cooking time.

4 To serve, heat the custard until it is piping hot and spoon over the bases of 4 warm dessert plates. Arrange 2 pear halves on each plate. Decorate with grated lemon rind and serve.

VARIATION

This recipe also works well if you use cooking apples. For alternative flavours, replace the cinnamon with ground ginger and serve the pears sprinkled with chopped stem ginger in syrup. Alternatively, use ground allspice and spoon over some warmed dark rum to serve.

Carrot & Ginger Cake

Serves 10 • CALORIES PER SERVING: 300 • FAT CONTENT PER SERVING: 10 G

INGREDIENTS

225 g/8 oz plain (all-purpose) flour
1 tsp baking powder
1 tsp bicarbonate of soda
2 tsp ground ginger
1/2 tsp salt
175 g/6 oz light muscovado sugar
225 g/8 oz carrots, grated
2 pieces stem ginger in syrup, drained and chopped
25 g/1 oz root (fresh) ginger, grated
60 g/2 oz seedless raisins
2 medium eggs, beaten
3 tbsp corn oil
juice of 1 medium orange

FROSTING:
225 g/8 oz low-fat soft cheese
4 tbsp icing (confectioner's) sugar
1 tsp vanilla essence (extract)

TO DECORATE:
grated carrot
stem (fresh) ginger
ground ginger

1 Preheat the oven to 180°C/350°F/Gas Mark 4. Grease and line a 20.5 cm/8 inch round cake tin (pan).

2 Sift the flour, baking powder, bicarbonate of soda, ground ginger and salt into a bowl. Stir in the sugar, carrots, stem ginger, root (fresh) ginger and raisins. Make a well in the centre of the dry ingredients.

3 Beat together the eggs, oil and orange juice, then pour into the centre of the well. Combine the ingredients together.

4 Spoon the mixture into the tin and smooth the surface. Bake in the oven for 1–1¼ hours until firm to the touch, or until a skewer inserted into the centre comes out clean. Cool in the tin (pan).

5 To make the frosting, place the soft cheese in a bowl and beat to soften. Sift in the icing (confectioner's) sugar and add the vanilla essence (extract). Stir well to mix.

6 Remove the cake from the tin (pan) and smooth the frosting over the top. Decorate and serve.

Mocha Swirl Mousse

Serves 4 • Calories per serving: 130 • Fat content per serving: 6.5 g

INGREDIENTS

- 1 tbsp coffee and chicory essence (extract)
- 2 tsp cocoa powder, plus extra for dusting
- 1 tsp low-fat drinking chocolate powder
- 150 ml/5 fl oz/$^{2}/_{3}$ cup half-fat crème fraîche, plus 4 tsp to serve (see Cook's Tip, below)
- 2 tsp powdered gelatine
- 2 tbsp boiling water
- 2 large egg whites
- 2 tbsp caster (superfine) sugar
- 4 chocolate coffee beans, to serve

1 Place the coffee and chicory essence (extract) in one bowl, and 2 tsp cocoa powder and the drinking chocolate in another bowl. Divide the crème fraîche between the 2 bowls and mix both until well combined.

2 Dissolve the gelatine in the boiling water and set aside. In a grease-free bowl, whisk the egg whites and sugar until stiff and divide this mixture evenly between the coffee and chocolate mixtures.

3 Divide the dissolved gelatine between the 2 mixtures and, using a large metal spoon, gently fold until well mixed.

4 Spoon small amounts of the 2 mousses alternately into 4 serving glasses and swirl together gently. Chill for 1 hour or until set.

5 To serve, top each mousse with 1 tbsp of crème fraîche, a chocolate coffee bean and a light dusting of cocoa powder.

COOK'S TIP

Traditional crème fraîche is soured cream and has a fat content of around 40 per cent. It is thick and has a slightly sour and nutty flavour. Lower fat versions have a reduced fat content and are slightly looser in texture, but they should be used in a low-fat diet only occasionally. If you want to use a lower fat alternative, a reduced fat, unsweetened yogurt or fromage frais would be more suitable.

Brown Sugar Pavlovas

Serves 4 • CALORIES PER SERVING: 170 • FAT CONTENT PER SERVING: 0.2 G

INGREDIENTS

2 large egg whites
1 tsp cornflour (cornstarch)
1 tsp raspberry vinegar
100 g/3 1/2 oz light muscovado sugar, crushed free of lumps
2 tbsp redcurrant jelly
2 tbsp unsweetened orange juice
150 ml/5 fl oz/3/4 cup low-fat natural fromage frais (unsweetened yogurt)
175 g/6 oz raspberries, thawed if frozen
rose-scented geranium leaves, to decorate (optional)

1 Preheat the oven to 150°C/300°F/Gas Mark 2. Line a large baking sheet (cookie sheet) with baking parchment. In a large, grease-free bowl, whisk the egg whites until very stiff and dry. Fold in the cornflour (cornstarch) and vinegar.

2 Gradually whisk in the sugar, a spoonful at a time, until the mixture is thick and glossy.

3 Divide the mixture into 4 and spoon on to the baking sheet (cookie sheet), spaced well apart. Smooth each into a round, about 10 cm/4 inch across, and bake in the oven for 40–45 minutes until lightly browned and crisp; let cool.

4 Place the redcurrant jelly and orange juice in a small pan and heat, stirring, until melted. Leave to cool for 10 minutes.

5 Using a palette knife (spatula), carefully remove each pavlova from the baking parchment and transfer to a serving plate. Top with fromage frais (unsweetened yogurt) and raspberries. Spoon over the redcurrant jelly mixture to glaze. Decorate and serve.

VARIATION

Make a large pavlova by forming the meringue into a round, measuring 18 cm/7 inches across, on a lined baking sheet (cookie sheet) and bake for 1 hour.

1

2

3

Citrus Meringue Crush

Serves 4 • Calories per serving: 195 • Fat content per serving: 0.6 g

INGREDIENTS

8 ready-made meringue nests
300 ml/$^1/_2$ pint/1 $^1/_4$ cups low-fat natural (unsweetened) yogurt
$^1/_2$ tsp finely grated orange rind
$^1/_2$ tsp finely grated lemon rind
$^1/_2$ tsp finely grated lime rind
2 tbsp orange liqueur or unsweetened orange juice

TO DECORATE:
sliced kumquat
lime rind, grated

SAUCE:
60 g/2 oz kumquats
8 tbsp unsweetened orange juice
2 tbsp lemon juice
2 tbsp lime juice
2 tbsp water
2–3 tsp caster (superfine) sugar
1 tsp cornflour (cornstarch) mixed with 1 tbsp water

1 Place the meringues in a clean plastic bag, seal the bag and using a rolling pin, crush the meringues into small pieces. Transfer to a mixing bowl.

2 Stir the yogurt, grated citrus rinds and the liqueur or juice into the crushed meringue. Spoon the mixture into 4 mini-basins, smooth over the tops and freeze for 1½–2 hours until firm.

3 To make the sauce, thinly slice the kumquats and place them in a small pan with the fruit juices and water. Bring gently to the boil and then simmer over a low heat for 3–4 minutes until the kumquats have just softened.

4 Sweeten with sugar to taste, stir in the cornflour (cornstarch) mixture and cook, stirring, until thickened. Pour into a small bowl, cover the surface with a layer of cling film (plastic wrap) and leave to cool – the film will help prevent a skin forming. Leave to chill.

5 To serve, dip the meringue basins in hot water for 5 seconds or until they loosen, and turn on to serving plates. Spoon over a little sauce, decorate with slices of kumquat and lime rind and serve immediately.

Banana & Lime Cake

Serves 10 • CALORIES PER SERVING: 360 • FAT CONTENT PER SERVING: 2.8 G

INGREDIENTS

300 g/10½ oz plain (all-purpose) flour
1 tsp salt
1½ tsp baking powder
175 g/6 oz light muscovado sugar
1 tsp lime rind, grated
1 medium egg, beaten
1 medium banana, mashed with 1 tbsp lime juice
150 ml/5 fl oz/⅔ cup low-fat natural fromage frais (unsweetened yogurt)
115 g/4 oz sultanas
banana chips and finely grated lime rind, to decorate

TOPPING:
115 g/4 oz icing (confectioner's) sugar
1–2 tsp lime juice
½ tsp lime rind, finely grated

1 Preheat the oven to 180°C/350°F/Gas Mark 4. Grease and line a deep 18 cm/7 inch round cake tin (pan) with baking parchment. Sift the flour, salt and baking powder into a bowl and stir in the sugar and lime rind.

2 Make a well in the centre of the dry ingredients and add the egg, banana, fromage frais (yogurt) and sultanas. Mix well until incorporated.

3 Spoon the mixture into the tin and smooth the surface. Bake for 40–45 minutes until firm to the touch or until a skewer inserted in the centre comes out clean. Leave to cool for 10 minutes, then turn out on to a wire rack.

4 For the topping, sift the icing (confectioner's) sugar into a bowl and mix with the lime juice to form a soft, but not too runny, icing. Stir in the lime rind. Drizzle the icing over the cake, letting it run down the sides.

5 Decorate with banana chips and lime rind. Let stand for 15 minutes so that the icing sets.

VARIATION

Replace the lime rind and juice with orange and the sultanas with chopped apricots.

1

2

3

Chocolate Cheese Pots

Serves 4 • Calories per serving: 170 • Fat content per serving: 3 g

INGREDIENTS

300 ml/½ pint/1¼ cups low-fat natural fromage frais (unsweetened yogurt)
150 ml/5 fl oz/⅔ cup low-fat natural (unsweetened) yogurt
25 g/1 oz icing (confectioner's) sugar
4 tsp low-fat drinking chocolate powder
4 tsp cocoa powder
1 tsp vanilla essence (extract)
2 tbsp dark rum (optional)
2 medium egg whites
4 chocolate cake decorations

TO SERVE:
pieces of kiwi fruit, orange and banana
strawberries and raspberries

1 Combine the fromage frais (unsweetened yogurt) and low-fat yogurt in a mixing bowl. Sift in the sugar, drinking chocolate and cocoa powder and mix well. Add the vanilla essence (extract) and rum, if using.

2 In another bowl, whisk the egg whites until stiff. Using a metal spoon, fold the egg whites into the fromage frais (unsweetened yogurt) and chocolate mixture.

3 Spoon the fromage frais (unsweetened yogurt) and chocolate mixture into 4 small china dessert pots and leave to chill for about 30 minutes. Decorate each chocolate cheese pot with a chocolate cake decoration.

4 Serve each chocolate cheese pot with an assortment of fresh fruit, such as pieces of kiwi fruit, orange and banana, and a few whole strawberries and raspberries.

VARIATION

This chocolate mixture would make an excellent filling for a cheesecake. Make the base out of crushed Amaretti di Saronno biscuits and egg white, and set the filling with 2 tsp powdered gelatine dissolved in 2 tbsp boiling water. Make sure you use biscuits made from apricot kernels, which are virtually fat free.

This is a Parragon Book
This edition published in 2003
Parragon
Queen Street House
4 Queen Street
Bath BA1 1HE, UK

ISBN: 1-40541-926-1

Printed in China

Note

Cup measurements in this book are for American cups. Tablespoons are assumed to be 15 ml. Unless otherwise stated, milk is assumed to be full fat, eggs are medium and pepper is freshly ground black pepper.